To Addy and Izzy,

Dad, What's it Called Again?

Pups, Hatchlings, Puggles and More!

love Grandma Karen

Written by **Ryan Hunka**

Illustrated by **Kiran Akram**

For my little Fox, I love you to the moon and beyond, forever and always. Thank you for the idea for this book.

–Dad

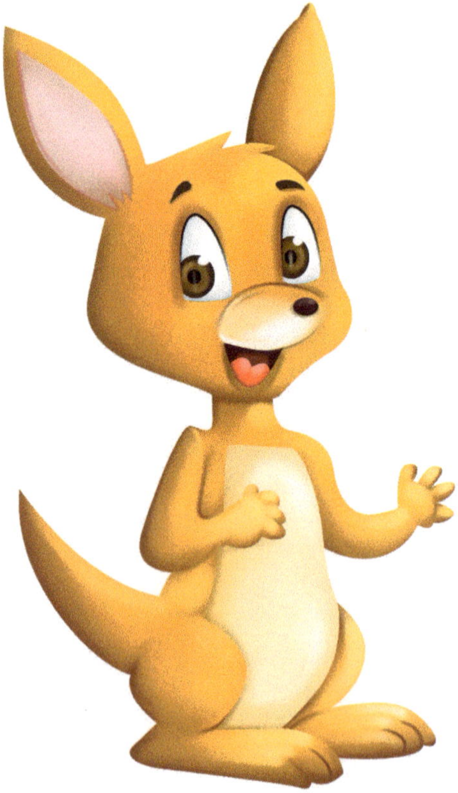

KANGAROO

**"Dad, what's it called again?
A baby kangaroo?"**

"It's called a joey.

They stay in their momma's pouches to stay warm and grow for six months. Kangaroos hop forward, but not backward. Their tail helps them balance and move, almost like having an extra arm or leg."

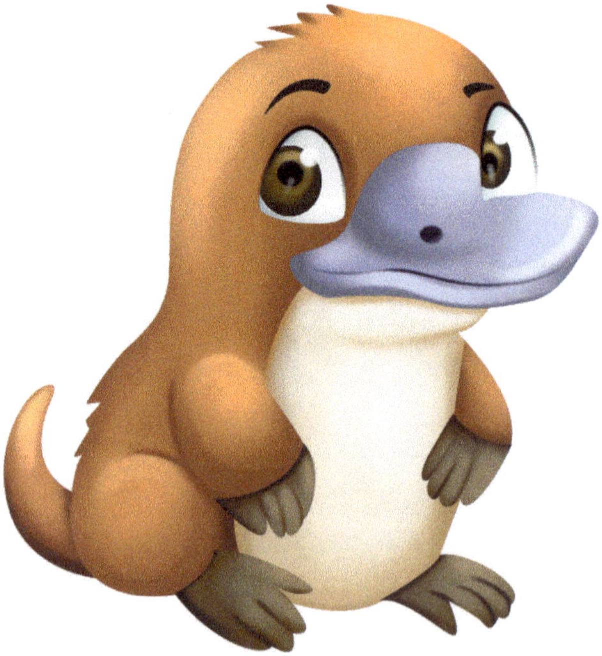

PLATYPUS

**"Dad, what's it called again?
A baby platypus?"**

"It's called a puggle.

It has teeny-tiny eyes, a flat head, and silky-smooth hair. They are one of the only mammals that lay eggs."

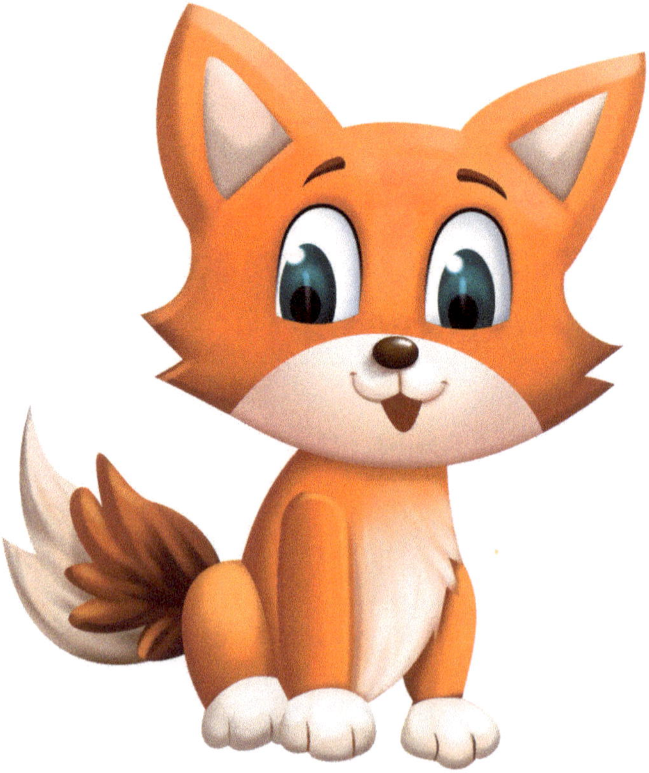

FOX

"Dad, what's it called again? A baby fox?"

"It's called a kit.

They are born with blue eyes, but they change to amber when they are about four to five weeks old. Foxes have incredible senses and can hear a mouse squeak from very far away."

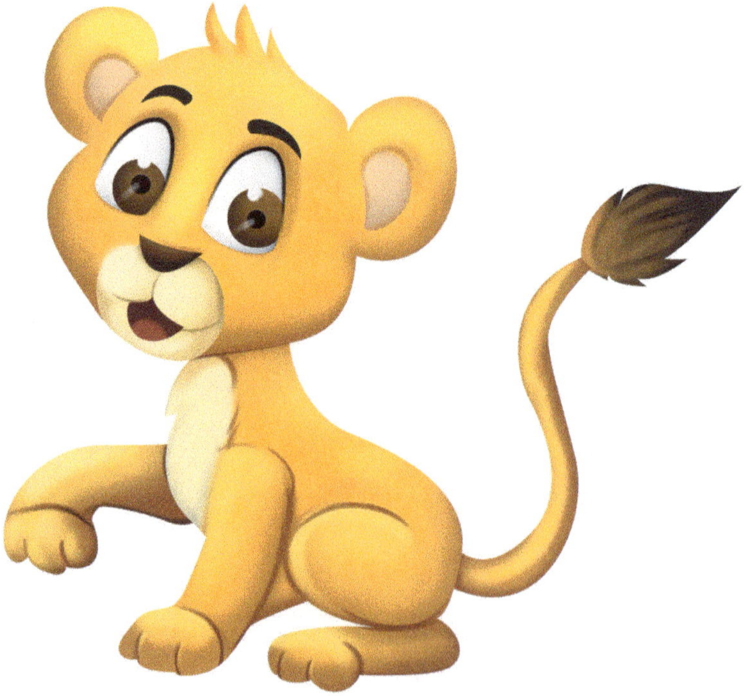

LION

**"Dad, what's it called again?
A baby lion?"**

"It's called a cub.

They are born without teeth. They grow small ones when they are a couple of months old. They start to walk when they are ten to fifteen days old. Lion cubs love to play."

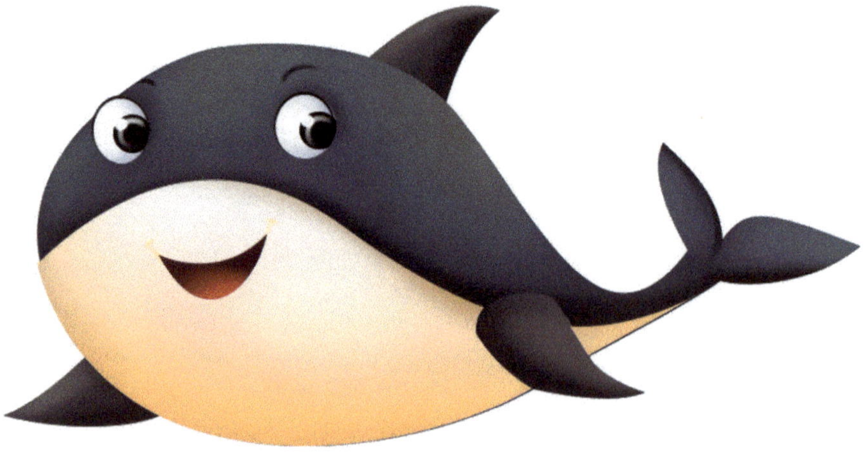

ORCA

**"Dad, what's it called again?
A baby orca?"**

"It's called a calf.

They are born a black and peachy-orange color instead of black and white. A newborn calf is seven to eight feet long, and they are able to swim and dive."

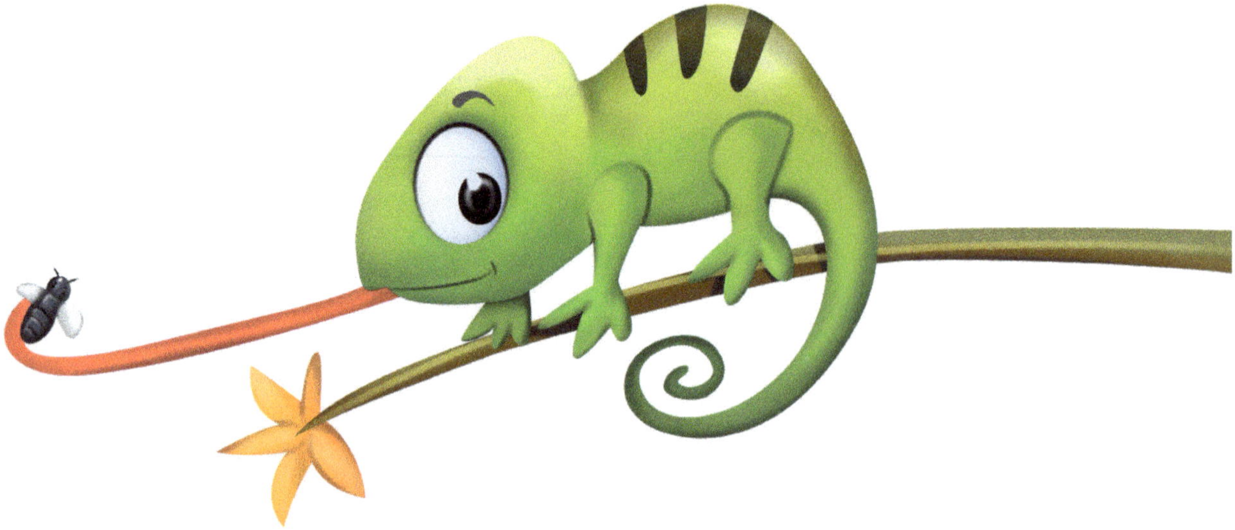

CHAMELEON

**"Dad, what's it called again?
A baby chameleon?"**

"It's called a *hatchling*.

They can walk within seconds of hatching from their egg. Chameleons have eyes that can move in different directions and long sticky tongues for catching food."

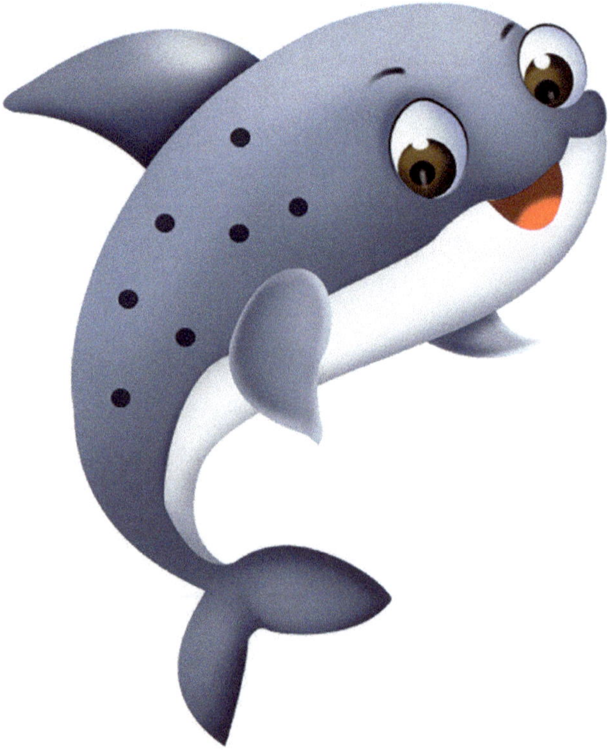

WHALE SHARK

**"Dad, what's it called again?
A baby whale shark?"**

"It's called a pup.

They are a shark, not a whale, and they grow to be the biggest fish in the sea. Whale sharks have scales that look like teeth on their eyes.
They can live to be over 100 years old!"

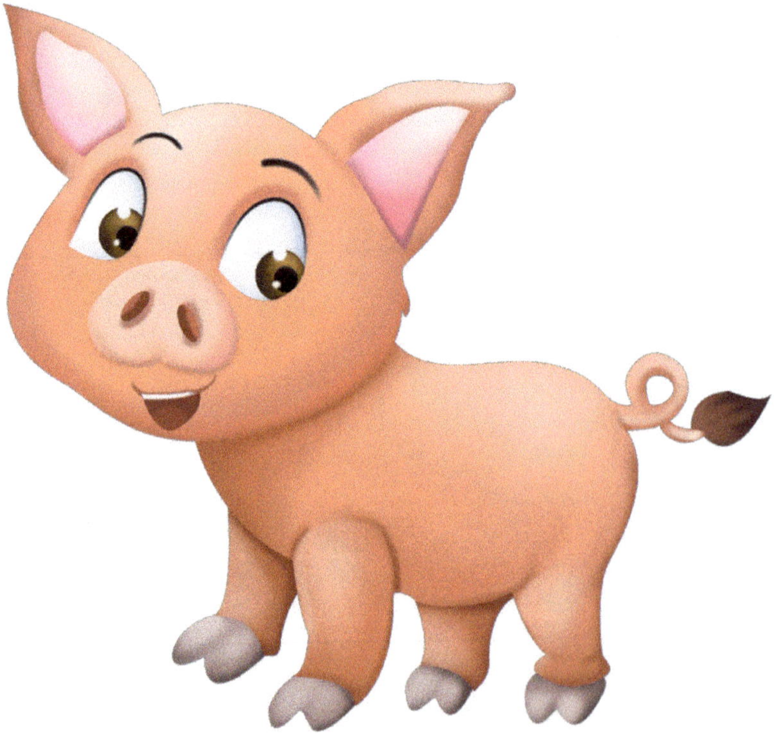

PIG

**"Dad, what's it called again?
A baby pig?"**

"It's called a piglet.

They learn to run towards their mothers' voices.
Pigs have over twenty distinct grunts and squeals.
A litter of piglets is called a farrow."

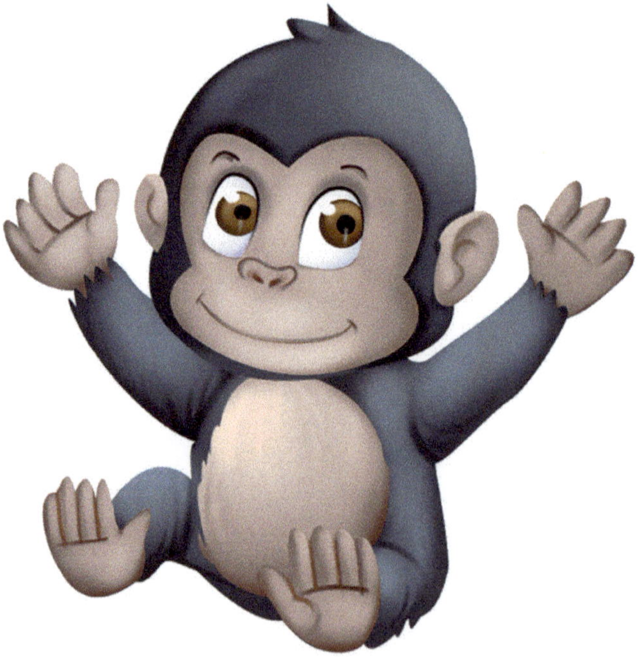

GORILLA

"Dad, what's it called again?
A baby gorilla?"

"It's called an **infant**.

They like to play, wrestle, and climb trees.
They can eat all day long.
Gorillas cozy up into family groups at night."

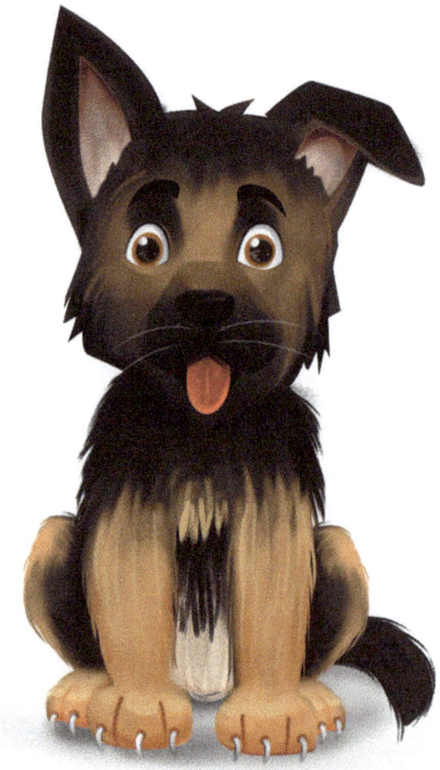

GERMAN SHEPHERD

**"Dad, what's it called again?
A baby German shepherd?"**

"It's called a puppy.

Their ears are floppy when they are born and then stand up when they are around eight to twelve weeks old. They are quick learners, and are playful and protective. They are very loyal.
German Shepherds love having a job to do."

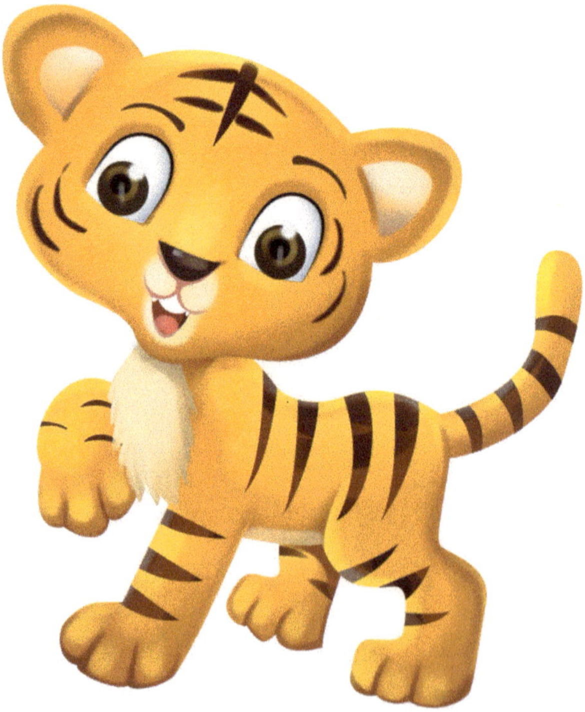

TIGER

**"Dad, what's it called again?
A baby tiger?"**

"It's called a cub.

They are born blind, so they are dependent on their mothers. Baby tigers have sharp baby teeth. They are very playful. They love to tumble around with their brothers and sisters, and they like to try and catch birds."

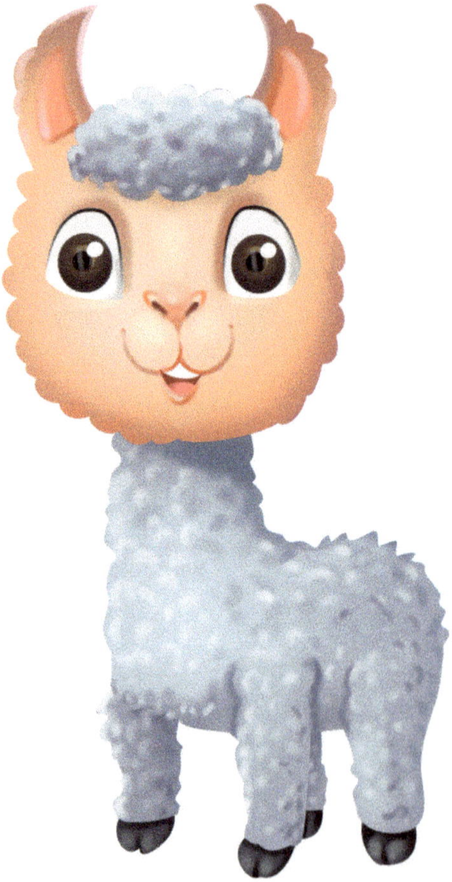

LLAMA

**"Dad, what's it called again?
A baby llama?"**

"It's called a Cria.

They are very smart and make excellent guards for herds of small animals. Llamas communicate by humming."

DUCK

**"Dad, what's it called again?
A baby duck?"**

"It's called a *duckling*.

They are born with a fluffy, fuzz-like covering instead of feathers. Their eyes are very special, as they can see three times as far as humans, and are able to see clearly underwater. Ducklings communicate with each other before hatching from their eggs."

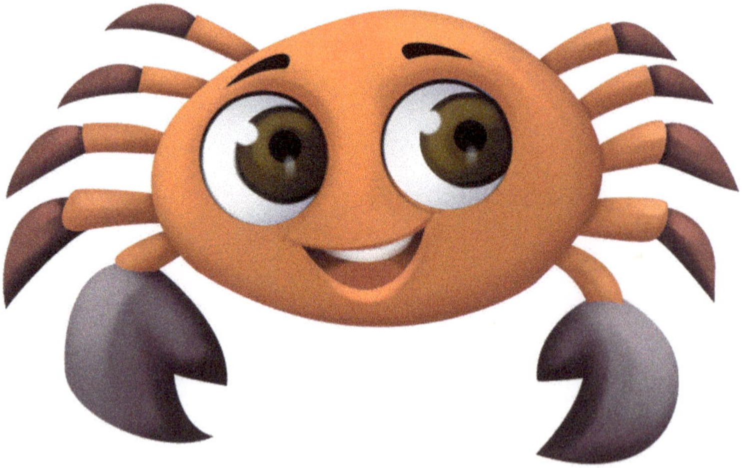

CRAB

**"Dad, what's it called again?
A baby crab?"**

"It's called a zoea.

They are decapods, which means ten-footed.
The first pair are actually it's claws, and are called
chelea. Crabs move by walking sideways,
and communicate by drumming
or waiving their pincers."

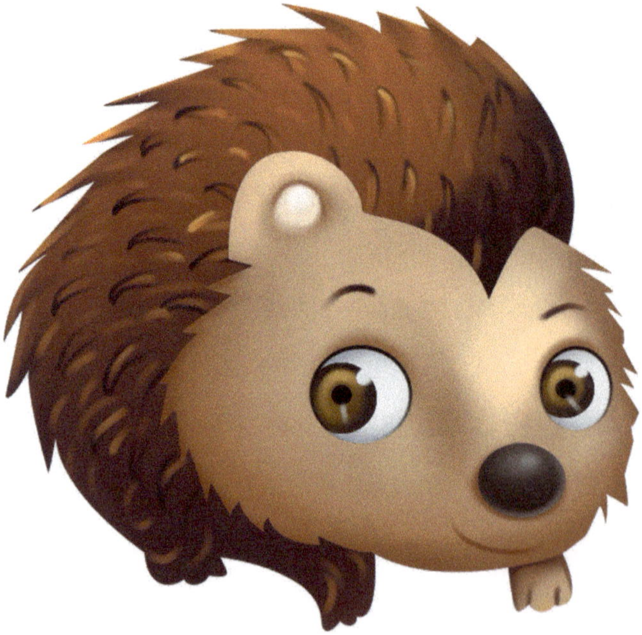

HEDGEHOG

**"Dad, what's it called again?
A baby hedgehog?"**

"It's called a hoglet.

They are born blind and deaf. When the hoglets are four weeks old, they are ready to start foraging for food. They are great climbers and runners. Hedgehogs are nocturnal, which means they are active at night."

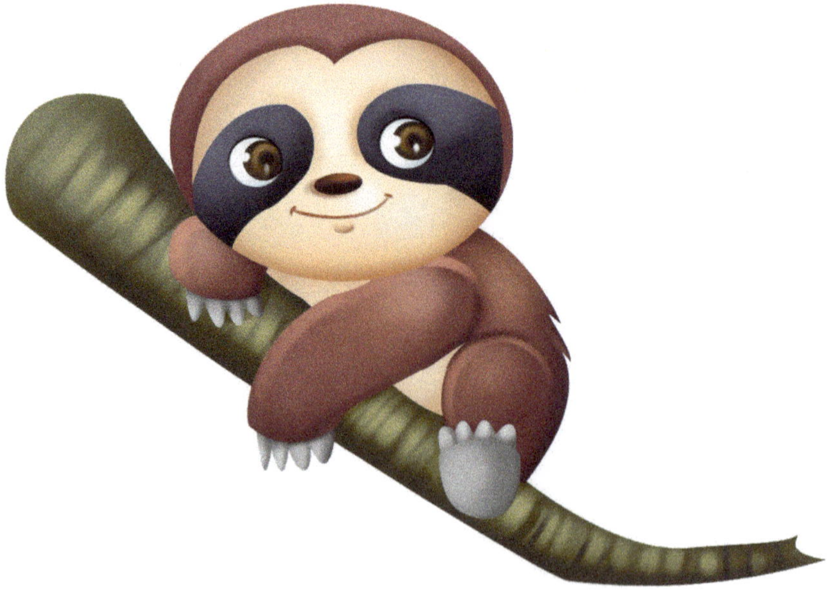

SLOTH

**"Dad, what's it called again?
A baby sloth?"**

"It's called a pup.

They are born with a full coat of hair,
their eyes open, and with all their teeth.
They have sharp claws and are able to climb,
although not too fast!"

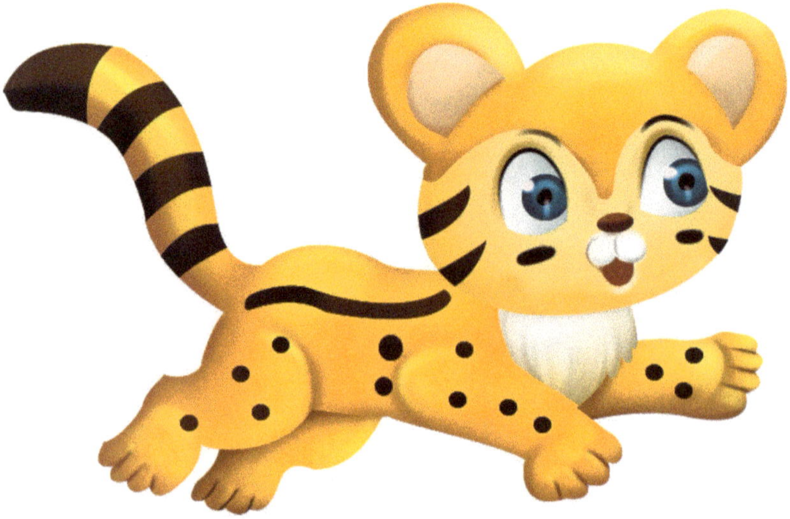

OCELOT

**"Dad, what's it called again?
A baby ocelot?"**

"It's called a kitten.

When the kittens are born, their fur is gray with spots, and they have blue eyes. After a few months their eyes turn golden brown.
Every ocelot's coat is unique.
They are nocturnal."

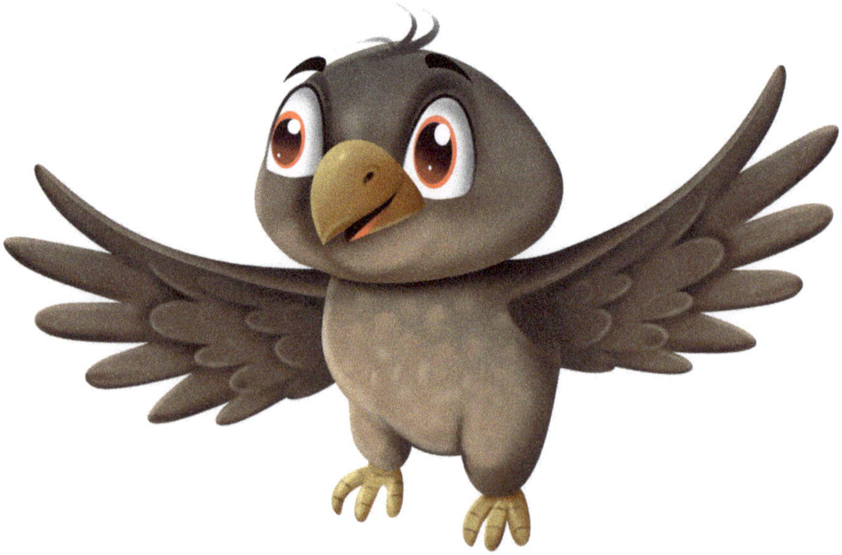

EAGLE

**"Dad, what's it called again?
A baby eagle?"**

"It's called an *eaglet*.

They bang or knock their beaks together to help develop their muscles and coordination. It also helps them decide who eats first, by competing for food and establishing the pecking order. Eaglets play tug of war and practice holding things in their talons."

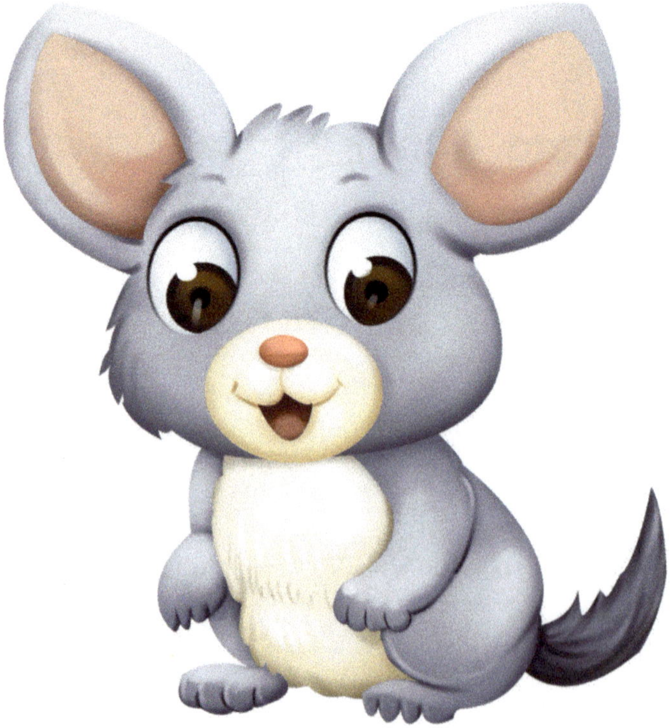

CHINCHILLA

"Dad, what's it called again?
A baby chinchilla?"

"It's called a kit.

They are born with big ears, soft fur,
and muscular hind legs for hopping around.
Chinchillas also have bushy tails
and quirky personalities."

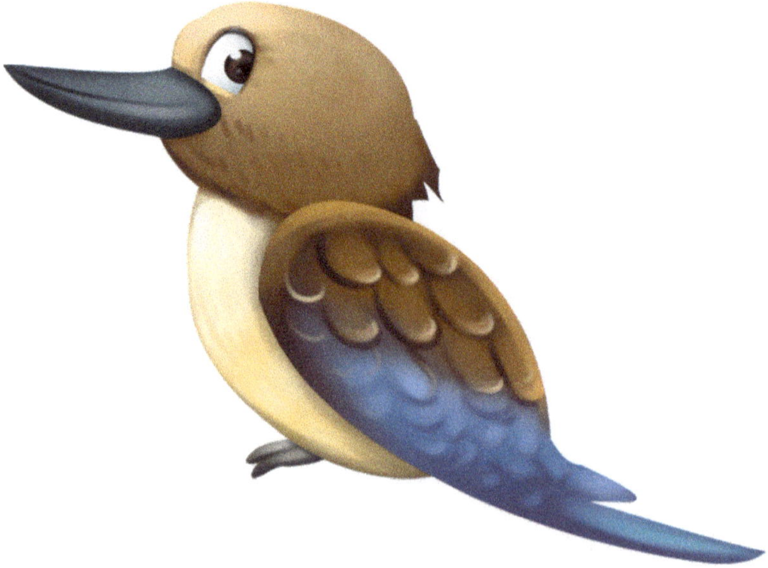

KOOKABURRA

**"Dad, what's it called again?
A baby kookaburra?"**

"It's called a chick.

They are born without feathers and are fed by their parents. Their call sounds like a human laughing. This laughing sound is how a kookaburra tells other birds that the area is theirs."

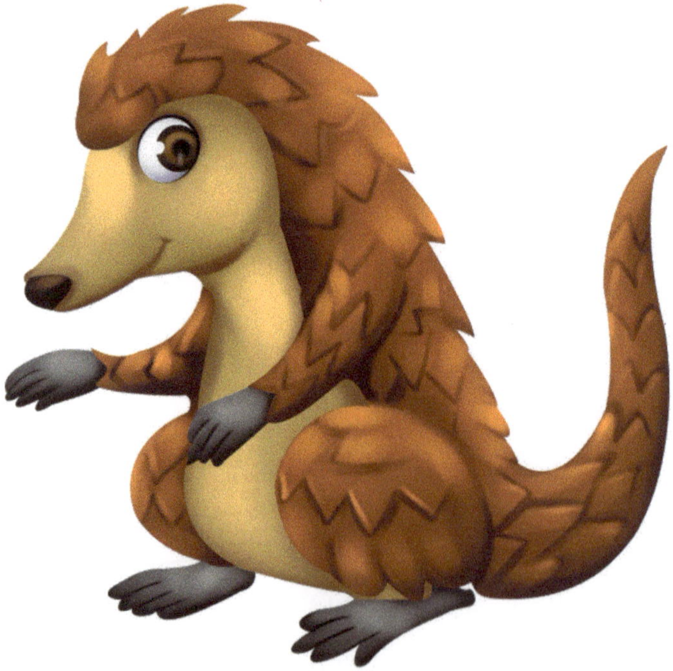

PANGOLIN

"Dad, what's it called again?
A baby pangolin?"

"It's called a **pangopup**.

They are born with soft white scales that harden after a few days. Pangolins catch insects with their sticky tongue. They curl into a ball and their hard scales protect them from predators."

ABOUT THE AUTHOR

Ryan Hunka is a proud dad living in Alberta, Canada. His inquisitive daughter inspires him daily with her endless questions about the world around her. This curiosity reignited his passion for writing, leading to his first children's book, *Dad, What's It Called Again?*, which explores the names of baby animals through their chats together. When he's not spending quality time with his daughter and their two German Shepherds, Ryan is committed to serving his community through his work with Fire Rescue Services.